ROWAN ATKINSON

ROWAN ATKINSON

● ● ● ● ● ● ● ●

Bruce Dessau

WELCOME RAIN

NEW YORK

ACKNOWLEDGMENTS

Many thanks to everyone too humorous to mention who assisted me in the compilation of this book. In particular many thanks to my employers *Time Out* and to Cath, Lily and Florence, who stayed out of my way when necessary and laughed at Rowan's jokes in all the right places when they were around.

PICTURE CREDITS

All Action/Splash   Big Pictures   Camera Press   Capital Pictures   Kobal Collection   London Features International   Mirror Syndication International   PA News   Pappix UK   Retna Pictures   Rex Features   Chris Ridley   Scope Features   © Snowdon/Camera Press   Frank Spooner Pictures © The Walt Disney Company/Kobal Collection

First WELCOME RAIN edition 1997
Published by WELCOME RAIN
New York, New York

Distributed by Stewart, Tabori & Chang
New York, New York

First published in 1997 by Orion Media
An imprint of Orion Books Ltd
Orion House, 5 Upper St Martin's Lane,
London WC2H 9EA

Copyright © Orion Books Ltd

Library of Congress cataloging information
is available from the publisher.

ISBN 1-55670-713-4

Colour reproduction by
Pixel Colour Ltd, London
Printed and bound in Great Britain by
Butler & Tanner Ltd, Frome and London

Contents

Nobody's Fool

● ● ● ● ● ● ● ● ● ● ● ●

California is full of strange people. It has been said that it is as if America has been tipped on one side and all the fruitcakes have slid down into the south-western corner. But on Venice Beach, a place where oddballs are a dime a dozen, one figure was attracting a disturbing amount of attention from assorted cyclists, joggers and rollerbladers. You couldn't miss him – while everyone else was sporting trunks and bikinis, he was wearing a tweed jacket and getting into difficulties with his skateboard. It was Mr Bean, or rather Rowan Atkinson, filming the first Mr Bean movie. Americans had embraced Rowan Atkinson. This didn't come as a surprise, but what did come as a surprise was that it took them so long. Rowan Atkinson has been a top-billing star for nearly two decades in Britain. America, after some false starts, has finally caught up with the quintessential modern clown.

OPPOSITE
Romance, Mr Bean style.

California Beaning: filming the movie in

Rowan Atkinson's roots are a world away from southern California. It might be easy to forget, given his Home Counties clothing and BBC accent, but coming from the north of England, Rowan Atkinson is a Geordie. He was born on 6 January 1955. His father, Eric, was a gentleman farmer, married to Ella May. They lived in Stocksfield, one of the swisher parts of the north-east – 'the Bel Air of Newcastle' – and used to commute down the A68 to Hole Row Farm, 12 miles south-west of Newcastle, overlooked by Consett steelworks. Rowan had two older brothers, Rodney and Rupert. With rigid middle-class efficiency he was also given a first name beginning with 'R'. Rowan Sebastian Atkinson. The middle name came from a character in Shakespeare's *Twelfth Night* – one of his farce-like comedies of errors.

As his brothers headed for predictable careers in finance, it looked as if Rowan would take over the farm. The young boy with the unruly mop of black hair was resigned to his inheritance, though every now and again he would wander around the grounds in the shadow of the nearby slag heaps, find himself coated in sinister red dust and wonder if this was what he wanted to be covered in for the next 50 years of his life.

His history seemed to have already determined his future at an early age. But behind the thoroughly respectable career ladder there was a spot of showbiz as well as entrepreneurialism in the Atkinson genes. Rowan's grandfather, Edward, had been the founder and owner of a chain of cinemas in the north-east, including the Empire in Consett, where Rowan would see the latest films. As a boy there was no television in the Atkinson household, but Rowan would visit his grandfather and watch television there. But actually being a part of the entertainment industry seemed like an impossible dream to young Rowan. He later recalled that 'acting was a strange job. Television was something people in the south did.' It was only when the young boy was 12 years old that his parents finally acquired a television. It was pretty good timing. It was the late '60s and BBC comedy was at its peak, with acutely scripted sitcoms such as *Steptoe And Son* and *Till Death Us Do Part*, followed briskly by the ensemble brilliance of *Dad's Army*. If there wasn't much humour to inspire him at home there certainly was plenty on the box.

'... and the Holy Goat': the definitive cameo in Four Weddings and a Funeral.

Early days at Durham School: Rowan Atkinson, top row right, Tony Blair, middle row left.

One comic stood head and shoulders above the others for the young Atkinson, in both a literal and a metaphorical sense. The gangly John Cleese had already made his mark in *The Frost Report*, in which invariably he would be cast as an upper-class bowler-hatted gent in satirical pieces. When *Monty Python's Flying Circus* came along, Cleese's resident toff continued, although there was a more surreal spin to it now. He might be playing a tuxedoed BBC announcer, but he would be behind a desk in a zoo or in a swamp; he might be an army officer, but he would be holding a fish. Most famously, he was a civil servant. He might have really been a civil servant in a parallel universe, but he would never have been employed by the Ministry of Silly Walks. Maybe in Cleese, Atkinson saw a potential comedy role model for someone from the middle classes. Cleese proved one could be a comedy superstar with received pronunciation and without spending one's formative years slogging around the working-men's clubs in the north of England.

When the bright pupil gained a scholarship to St Bees, a public school on the Cumbrian coast, there was little about him that marked him out for greatness. Admittedly he soon learned to recite *Monty Python* sketches verbatim, but by the early '70s *Python* was virtually a compulsory subject at British public schools, so it was hardly a unique selling point.

Then again, Atkinson did stand out in a crowd. By his early teens his appearance marked him out. His features became more prominent: his eyes bulged, his ears stuck out and his lips and nose seemed to go on for ever. His nostrils seemed wider than the Mersey Tunnel. It was as if puberty was making him mutate into a comic character. Or maybe it had something to do with the fact that St Bees was in such close proximity to the Windscale nuclear reactor. Whatever the reasons, it earned Atkinson a collection of affectionate nicknames – Dopie, Zoonie, Moonman, Green Man and Gruman – all stemming from the fact that his friends felt that he looked like an alien.

It has become a cliché in comedy biographies to pinpoint pivotal events in the comedian's early life. The usual canard trotted out is that the comic was bullied and used jokes to deflect punches and kicks like some kind of quick-witted verbal Superman. Unfortunately in Atkinson's case there seems to be little evidence that he was picked on any more than any other gawky adolescent. His comic genius was simply in there waiting to come out. It just emerged in the changing rooms when he was about 12. Jumping

As Atkinson's adolescence progressed, however, there weren't that many outward signs of future fame. He appeared in plays, but so did many of his peers at Durham Cathedral Choristers' School, a place staffed by the kind of mad vicars who would help to shape Atkinson's uniquely bizarre view of the clergy, perpetuated in his character in *Four Weddings and a Funeral*. He was also interested in being in a rock band, but this was the '60s and inevitably so were many of his peers (one of whom was Tony Blair).

Jacques Tati: the French film star made a career out of his funny features – not surprisingly Atkinson knew Monsieur Hulot's Holiday **backwards.**

up and down, pulling faces, he entertained his classmates and found the ensuing laughter not unsatisfying. His family, on the other hand, were dismissive of this new habit, assuming it was just a phase he was going through.

But no, he didn't immediately set his heart on a glittering showbiz career. There were exams to pass and qualifications to acquire. And, of course, it simply wasn't done for someone with his breeding to become a comedian. On the other hand, there was a bit of an epiphany when he was working on the lighting for a school play, as he recalled in *The Observer* in 1984: 'I remember looking down from the lighting gantry on to the stage during the performance and thinking, I've made the wrong decision – I'd prefer to be down there.'

Yet the theatre still seemed to take second place to making mischief.

Atkinson became one of those pupils who cleverly manages to straddle misbehaviour and academic achievement. He was an active member of the school, running the film society with Paddy Rickerby for two years. One of his favourite films was *Monsieur Hulot's Holiday*, starring French physical comic Jacques Tati. He once watched it seven times in one weekend and by the Monday morning knew every one of Tati's twitches and tics off by heart.

Atkinson's schoolroom results were impressive and his smoking was reportedly prodigious. Although he gave up tobacco in adulthood, as a teenager he could have smoked for England. Retribution was swift and severe if caught – a £1-fine paid to the Marie Curie Cancer Memorial Fund – and in one week, Atkinson was caught more times than anybody else.

Despite his good record in class, his behaviour outside almost got him expelled: although an innocent bystander, he was nearly linked to a drug-related scandal. Once he was given detention because he was told to pull his socks up and innocently followed the instructions literally. One form of punishment at St Bees was to pick up horse droppings from the school paddock. According to Atkinson only the privileged few were given shovels.

A public-school upbringing was filled with character-building activities: edifying but unenjoyable ordeals to be

A funny turn at the Queen Mother's Ninetieth Birthday Gala.

Making a meal of it in The Nerd.

gone through if you wanted to be a captain of industry. One of the toughest tasks for Atkinson was the 24-hour exercise at summer camp when, as a member of the cadet force, he had to stand on the rainy Cumbrian moors in a trench on guard duty from 8pm to 2am. After one hour he was soaked through. After two he was standing in a foot of water. His only solace was a non-filter Park Drive cigarette, but he couldn't light that because the Swan Vesta matches were soaked through too. It is not difficult to see from where Atkinson got his ambivalent feelings about authority.

He later recalled that his headmaster called him 'just about the most bloody-minded individual' he'd ever had in his charge. Their relationship seemed antagonistic, but it did reap results. The headmaster bet Atkinson that he wouldn't get an English O-level, but this only provoked the pupil to pass with flying colours.

Anecdotes about his schooldays certainly suggest that he had a nasty streak and a tendency to play cruel tricks on people who wronged him. There was one master with whom Rowan and his friends were particularly annoyed. According to later stories they got their revenge by teaching the teacher's toddler how to say 'fuck off'. It was not malicious, just an ingenious schoolboy prank, revealing already a sense of humour that was more about sophisticated cunning plans than rudimentary custard pies.

As an adult, Atkinson was unapologetic about the dark side of his schooldays because he didn't feel he had done anything wrong: 'I never meant any harm or offence to anyone – I was just trying to enjoy myself. Because, make no mistake, life is short.' A contemporary described Atkinson as being 'the one who is always kept behind after lessons and gets his revenge by writing scurrilous verse in Latin about the master who kept him in'.

Strangely Atkinson would later find these incidents and others increasingly amusing. Schooldays took on that inevitable rosy glow of nostalgia and as an adult he said that gathering with old friends could 'make me laugh more than I do at anything else in the world'. Memories of being forced to eat large plates of plain macaroni and unfluffy mashed potato at his primary school suddenly seemed more hilarious than ever.

Despite the odd excursion into drama, as a sinister head waiter, Mephistopheles, in Christopher Marlowe's *Dr Faustus* and the Dauphin in George Bernard Shaw's *St Joan*, Atkinson seemed to be more interested in work than plays. There was a reticence about being in the limelight that still lingers today. When he did take part in revues, though, he always ended up as the star of the show and his contributions were eagerly anticipated. When he was about to leave school, he finally received a glowing endorsement from his headmaster, who was more used to sending his charges off towards careers in business and the city. In Atkinson's case, however, he revealed that he had been quietly impressed by the young man's comic skills, remarking that 'I have never

A face, a piece of paper and a new routine is born.

recommended to anyone that they should take up a career in the entertainment industry, but it would seem silly for you, Atkinson, not at least to try …' The teenager, on the other hand, seemed less committed. Many years later he told *Woman's World* about his lack of focus: 'I didn't know quite what I wanted to do when I left. But I certainly didn't have very high expectations of the future.'

Beyond the school gates his interests veered towards the scientific. At home and on the farm he would spend hours tinkering with machinery and polishing tractors. Even before he was old enough to take his driving test – and it took him three times to pass when he did – he had learnt about motor mechanics by taking apart his mother's old Morris Minor, which she didn't want any more. Having fixed it he would spend hours tootling around his family's private land. He even customised it by crowbarring the wings off it. In a similar fashion he would later strip down comedy to its basic components when he created Mr Bean.

Not surprisingly this fascination with nuts and bolts, combined with a growing fondness for the stage, helped to determine the next step in his education. Atkinson decided that more qualifications might enhance his c.v. Following his A-levels, he decided to do a drama course in Portsmouth, albeit concentrating on the technical side. The lure of the greasepaint seemed to be getting to him.

Soon, however, he was back in the north-east, heading for Newcastle University to study for a B.Sc. in Electrical and Electronic Engineering.

Once again, his performing ambitions appeared to have taken a back seat to his scientific pursuits. He would still take part in revues, but he didn't seem to be trying to do anything special with his very special talents. Instead he would just do old comedy routines, remarking that there wasn't much point trying to come up with new material when there were 'the classics' to perform. His creative energies went into his studies. When he graduated he was still only 20 years old and he gained the highest marks in his year.

Instead of finding a job in preparation for taking over the running of his father's farm, Atkinson chose to remain in academia. If any one decision can be seen to have altered dramatically the course of his life it was this. Having spent most of his formative years in the north and not quite fitting in, he went to Queen's College, Oxford, to study for an M.Sc. in Engineering Science. It was the right place and the right time.

Or rather, it was nearly the right place at nearly the right time. The pre-eminent seat of learning for aspiring comics was still Cambridge, which could boast John Cleese among its past alumni, and David Baddiel and Emma Thompson among its future stars. The Oxford revue wasn't too bad a place to start out, though. And it soon helped that after a first term spent going to organ recitals Atkinson met up with some like-minded undergraduates, with whom he would form lasting friendships. Until now he had been funny with old material; now he had the nucleus of a creative team that would stand him in great stead

A major star even in a Mini: Atkinson filming Bean **outside Harrods.**

17

Comedy ambassador: Atkinson with Richard Curtis in the 'Drinks at the White House' sketch from his West End Revue.

well into his professional career: Richard Curtis, a sandy-haired bespectacled English student, also schooled in *Python* lore and with a love of verbal comedy, and Howard Goodall, a likeable music scholar with a ready wit. The threesome got on well. Curtis's early recollections of Atkinson are of a shy quiet postgraduate. Curtis thought Atkinson was so unobtrusive when they were gathered in a room that he likened him to a cushion.

Atkinson's comedy career at Oxford was hardly backed by anything so vulgar as driving ambition, but underneath the quiet exterior there was clearly a need to perform. He later recalled that 'there was something inside me crying to get out.' While other students mounted their own plays and booked rehearsal rooms with frantic enthusiasm, Atkinson's big break was more modest, though incredibly swift. In 1976, still in his first year at Queen's, Atkinson saw an advert pinned on a board asking for people to audition. This was no road-to-Damascus moment: he simply thought he would have a go. Having landed a part, he warmed up by pulling faces in front of a mirror. It was the first time he had done it for many years and he was quite amazed at the looks he could achieve. Perhaps this was the reason his comedy at Newcastle had been so unoriginal – it wasn't just the lack of words, he hadn't yet found his own face. Now that he pulled faces and got a laugh he realised why he hadn't done it for so long. It was that class thing again; as he said many years later in *The*

Daily Telegraph, 'I don't think it was a time when people who pulled faces were admired.' Not surprisingly, given his ambivalent feelings about this unique gift, he would spend as much of his career fleeing from his face as capitalising on its extraordinary elasticity.

It was the mid '70s, the country was in the economic doldrums, with strikes and working to rule decimating British industry and paving the way for Margaret Thatcher's election and subsequent revolution in 1979. He applied to the BBC to be a sound engineer but was turned down. Had he been accepted, the funniest visual comic on television might now be working anonymously behind the cameras, not starring in front of them.

In 1976 he, Goodall and Curtis decided to try their luck at the Edinburgh Fringe Festival, squeezing themselves and their equipment into Rowan's Volkwagen camper van and heading up the motorway. By now Atkinson was a bit of a veteran of the Fringe Festival, having performed there twice as a schoolboy, firstly in *The Fire Raisers* and secondly in *We Bombed Newhaven* by Joseph Heller. The first show was a success; the second did less well, because the author of *Catch 22* was not quite such a big attraction this time round.

Once again Atkinson's timing with the Oxford show wasn't quite right. Edinburgh had yet to become the media Mecca where television commissioning editors would snap up all the tickets and sign up the best acts for lengthy series before the applause had died down. Then again Atkinson and Co. were able to turn this to their advantage. Performing between the lazy dross that passed for satire and the drugged-up performance art that was comedy's version of lumpen progressive rock, Atkinson's performance swept the board. It also helped that he had had the definitive cunning plan. In order to attract attention to the show, he had written to nine London agents.

Off-duty but dutifully pulling an obligatory funny face.

One of them, Richard Armitage, who was John Cleese's agent, happened to be charmed by the way the letter started by saying 'Dear Sir or Madam'. He flew up, saw the show, was duly impressed and became Atkinson's agent. A couple of things that stood out, Armitage later recalled, were that when the other members of the cast went off at the end, Atkinson stayed on and the applause continued, and also that only once in the show did he speak in normal English. According to Armitage, 90 per cent of his act had been mime.

As for the rest of the Atkinson family, they were beginning to realise that this performance thing was more than just a phase their son was going through. The farm would obviously have to manage without him, but his mother was still anxious about this show-business lark. Recalling the turning point in the early part of his career, the young comic later said that 'she thought it was full of bouncing cheques and homosexuals and people in nasty bow-ties, so I got a really well-dressed middle-class agent who looked like a bank manager and that reassured her a lot'.

With John Cleese: the former hero soon became a colleague – and boss – as Atkinson appeared in Cleese's managerial advice films made by his company Video Arts.

A Partly Political Broadcast

● ● ● ● ● ● ● ● ● ●

T wenty years on it is hard to convey quite how quickly Rowan Atkinson became a star. But to put it into perspective it is worth comparing his career to that of his hero John Cleese. The Python lynchpin went through the Footlights, graduated, did other bits of television and became a name in his own right with *Fawlty Towers* in the mid '70s. It took John Cleese around 15 years to become a household name. Rowan Atkinson had a BBC Radio 3 series, *The Atkinson People*, while still at Oxford, a solo London show a year later and was confident enough to turn down an ITV series a year after that following a successful pilot. A year later he was appearing alongside John Cleese and assorted other Pythons in the 'Four Yorkshiremen' sketch at *The Secret Policeman's Ball*. You don't need to be a rocket scientist – or an electronic engineer for that matter – to work out that Rowan Atkinson's rise was nothing short of meteoric.

**Cartoon clown: Atkinson as
'the Nerd' in Larry Shue's play.**

Even more remarkably, some of Atkinson's most famous work was already fully formed by the time his Edinburgh show came to London's Hampstead Theatre in 1978. *Beyond a Joke* – an unwitting homage to that other classic student revue, *Beyond the Fringe* – was acclaimed by all who saw it. Some people went back every night if they could get a ticket. By now John Cleese himself had seen Atkinson and was suitably impressed, remarking that 'I was very intrigued. He's very, very good.' Even when the gags were weak he felt that the performer was strong: 'He was making people laugh with some material I'd have paid money to avoid.'

Peter Cook also saw *Beyond a Joke* and described its star thus: 'It is impossible not to be funny when you are around the man. He's positively inspiring.' The satirist would later team up with Atkinson to play King Richard III in *The Black Adder* and would get beheaded by the young upstart for his pains.

Among the various authority figures lampooned in *Beyond a Joke* it was Atkinson's version of a public school headmaster reading the register that captured the audience's imagination. As the names became increasingly absurd and abstract they also became increasingly sinister: 'Aynsley … Babcock … Bland … Carthorse … Nibble … come on, settle down … Orifice … Plectrum …', all the way through the alphabet to 'Zob … absent'. But it wasn't just the student surrealism of the words, or even the perfect pauses in between each name. It was the way Atkinson said them. His full lips could make a short, tiny word like 'Nibble' resonate for ever, or make a long word like 'Witcherlywilliams-Wockett' last only a nanosecond. It is a unique verbal skill, which, welded to a face that one critic described as 'Peter Lorre in a panic', became a truly memorable piece of comedy.

One of the other members of the media scrum at the Hampstead Theatre was Humphrey Barclay, an ITV producer. He signed Atkinson and his writers up to make a pilot for the mainstream channel. *Canned Laughter* was the first television showcase of Atkinson's talents and to all concerned his live persona transferred pretty well to the box; verbal gags, physical gags and downright farce all translated very effectively. The camera seemed to love the contorted expressions and, if anything, make them even more grotesque. In one unforgettable sequence, Atkinson played a man who is late leaving his flat in the morning. To save time he spoons the instant coffee straight into his mouth, adds milk and sugar, and then, as the ultimate *coup de théâtre*, finishes off the scene by pouring boiling water from the kettle straight down his gullet. *Canned Laughter* was memorable because it – and Atkinson – was so unquantifiable. It wasn't slapstick and yet it was. It wasn't undergraduate humour and yet it was. Atkinson was an instant star and yet he also had huge potential. In the comedy world at least, this posh yet exotic-looking chap seemed to be capable of every kind of joke.

Only six months out of university, Rowan Atkinson had appeared in

countless households even if he wasn't quite a household name. Yet when Humphrey Barclay offered him the chance of an ITV series he declined. Success had come quickly and he didn't appear to want to rush into things. If there has been a constant in Rowan Atkinson's professional career it is that he has always taken each step cautiously. On stage it might be hilarious to see a clown fall flat on his face; off stage, in professional terms, it can be a disaster. One bad career move could ruin everything, so despite the chance of a solo television show, Atkinson held back, looking for a more anonymous way of marketing his very distinctive talents.

In the summer of 1979 there was an opportunity to showcase some of his best material in front of the greatest comics of his generation. *The Secret Policeman's Ball* at Her Majesty's Theatre in London was a precursor of Comic Relief, gathering together show-business names in aid of a good cause. This summer the cause was Amnesty International, though most of the people who went to these shows were probably there more to see the likes of Victoria Wood, Billy Connolly, the *Beyond the Fringe* team and sundry Pythons than to support human rights.

Atkinson may have been the new boy but his talents certainly justified his inclusion. Once again, it was the headmaster sketch, now taking on classic status of dead-parrot-like proportions, that earned him the most rapturous applause. When he came on with John Cleese, Michael Palin and Terry Jones to do the 'Four Yorkshiremen' sketch

('By God we 'ad it tough ...') the response from the audience was a mixture of disbelief and awe. On the one hand how could this upstart with the rubber face share stage space with these comedy gods? It was like someone from the Bay City Rollers duetting with Bob Dylan. Then again there was admiration that Atkinson managed to pull it off, bluff Yorkshire accent and all, and fit in. If there was any comedy baton-passing to be done, it was done that night – this was the ultimate endorsement of Atkinson's talents. The Oxbridge mafia was alive and well and on stage at Her Majesty's Theatre.

Atkinson consolidated his reputation with *The Secret Policeman's Ball*, and he made it soon after when he started filming the BBC series he chose in preference to his own ITV show. Having failed to get a job there as a sound engineer, clearly he bore Auntie no malice.

Of the original line-up of *Not the Nine O'Clock News* first screened in April 1979 only Atkinson would survive when the series made it big. John Gorman of comedy pop group the Scaffold and children's television show *Tiswas* was in the original line-up, as were Chris Emmett, Christopher Godwin and Jonathan Hyde; Chris Langham – almost as odd-looking as Atkinson – made it as far as the first series before going on to greater things, including working with the Muppets and Jonathan Ross. BBC producer John Lloyd had been looking for a group of comics to bring back satire and Atkinson had been just what he needed. Two other Oxbridge graduates, Mel Smith and

Griff Rhys Jones, soon joined the ranks and also got their first major television breaks here, as did a young Australian comedy actress, Pamela Stephenson, whose roles until then had invariably been as the token sexy woman in inept British movies. After a faltering start the series was destined to be a huge hit.

Although they were a contrived group, as manufactured as the Spice Girls, there was an undeniable chemistry among the quartet. Griff Rhys Jones was

With Mel Smith, colleague-turned-director for The Tall Guy **and** Bean.

27

the lantern-jawed cynic; Mel Smith was the maniacal hippy; Stephenson revealed a genuine facility for comic impressions; and Atkinson just kept doing what he had been doing in his solo shows and on *Canned Laughter*. The series was irreverent and pacy, managing to combine the intelligence of *Monty Python* with accessibility and a healthy lack of élitisism. The comedy was political but broad. Footage would be shown of Iranians bowing down to Mecca *en masse* and a spoof *BBC News* voiceover would announce that in Iran the search was continuing for the Ayatollah's contact lens. The cult of the pop video was sent up with the quartet hamming it up as new romantics singing 'Nice Video, Shame about the Song'.

Atkinson's distinctive features – distinctive even among the most odd-looking comedy ensemble ever gathered together for a television series – singled him out as the star. One of his new characters, known simply as the Ranting Man, also became something of a national celebrity. Like Peter Cook's E.L. Wisty on speed cross-bred with Mary Whitehouse, Atkinson's invention would be lurking in the studio audience inside his mac and at an unexpected point would stand up to protest at something that was annoying him. He was Disgusted of Tunbridge Wells gone mad, and there was, Atkinson conceded, some of himself in there too.

The success of *Not the Nine O'Clock News* was swift. Hailed as the funniest comedy show in many years, it even had to be moved to 9.30pm

The 'NTNON' team reunite. Note Atkinson's Blackadder **producer John Lloyd, second from right.**

STAN LAUREL AND OLIVER HARDY-Metro-Goldwyn-Mayer

MG-15

because in those pre-video days there were so many arguments between family members: some wanted to watch the real *BBC News*, while others preferred this partly political broadcast on behalf of the Daft Party.

By 1980 Rowan Atkinson was public property and he had mixed feelings about it. Although perfectly relaxed with his friends, he was uncomfortable about the fame factor and its paradoxes. Attention on stage was one thing but attention off it was another. Then again, his logical mind had computed the viewing figures and told him that he ought to be even more anxious if people didn't recognise him off screen.

Faced with the double-edged sword of celebrity, Atkinson agreed to be interviewed by the press but found the experience difficult. A stammer, which would disappear during performance, would return when he was put under the spotlight by probing journalists eager to categorise him. The *Guardian* visited his Camden Town house and commented on its sparseness, noticing little more than ordered filing cabinets and a huge Laurel and Hardy photograph in which the silent comedians were moping around. The paper concluded that Atkinson was the definitive anal retentive sad-eyed clown. It didn't allow for the fact that he had only just moved into the house and had been too busy to furnish it. (The journalist also noticed a summons for wilfully riding a bike along a footpath – the naughty schoolboy was still not averse to a minor spot of bad behaviour.)

By now Atkinson was well aware that he had become a comedy star by a relatively little trodden path. He had never done what one would call stand-up comedy. Even in his live solo shows he didn't really tell what you could call jokes, or even stories. Like a one-man old-fashioned revue with an '80s anarchism he simply created little characters and vignettes for the audience to chuckle at. When journalists would ask him to describe himself, he was keen to say 'character actor' or 'performer with a comic bias'. If you wanted to get on his wrong side all you had to do was call him a 'comic'. In the *Daily Mirror* he was already looking for ways of breaking out of the funny face mould: 'I'd rather like the Woody Allen idea – he's a tragic character who plays it funny. I certainly see that as a sort of stage two in my career.' He even saw a future playing tragedy where other funny men had played the fool: 'Perhaps I have a slightly better chance of playing Hamlet than Ken Dodd,' he joked.

Even Atkinson's off-stage pursuits set him apart from his peers. There was no celebrity golf, just truck driving. Having got into mechanics tinkering about with the equipment on his father's farm, he now liked lorries more than ever (he even sent up his hobby on *Not the Nine O'Clock News* with a musical homage to the sexy Yorkie Man ads of the day with the innuendo-laden hook-line of 'I like truckin' and I like to truck'). Still a technician at heart, he told *The Observer* with great pride that he had helped build his Edinburgh Festival stage, but he was proudest of all of having passed his HGV test; he could now drive modest-sized trucks on

Laurel and Hardy: classic clowns who inspired a contemporary clown.

the open road himself and talked earnestly of the possibility of packing in performance and setting up a theatrical trucking agency. He felt there was nothing better than being out on the open road in the cab of a juggernaut all on one's own, although he was also partial to fast cars and still in his mid 20s was already awaiting delivery of his first Aston Martin. 'I've always been a bit of a loner and lorry driving is a loner's dream,' he told the *Daily Mail*. 'I love the sense of power and responsibility. I suppose it reveals a suppressed megalomania.'

At home with a Ferrari.

    Atkinson was an exceptional star in all sorts of ways. Many performers are introverted when the stage lights go out, but Atkinson went further than most

in keeping his private life separate. He had no girlfriend to speak of, he had only just moved out of a friend's house in Kilburn, where he had been a lodger, and was now living on his own; he confessed that despite being a superb physical comic, he was too shy to play charades, even with friends. He was an extreme case study of the classic introverted extrovert, preferring to perform in front of eight million people rather than mime a film title in front of eight.

As the '70s turned into the '80s it was a strange time for Atkinson. Apart from his *Not the Nine O'Clock News* colleagues, and Curtis and Goodall, there seemed to be very few people on his wavelength. Atkinson was now known as

Buster Keaton: a comic influence who also had some run-ins with motor vehicles.

Chaplin: the first comedy superstar of stage and screen. Was Mr Bean a distant descendant of the Little Tramp?

someone who could be anarchic and unpredictable but also amazingly controlled. Physically he seemed able to get into positions no ordinary human body should have been capable of. He seemed to have more joints than was fair. Despite this remarkable facility for physical humour, however, he would still get nervous before a live performance, sitting silently for 45 minutes before going on stage.

When people met Atkinson for the first time they were surprised how the putty-faced performer could look so gloomy in repose. Yet one only had to think back to the films he used to book for the St Bees film society – silents by Buster Keaton, Charlie Chaplin, talkies by Laurel and Hardy and the more recent Jacques Tati – to see where the hangdog look came from. And there was also that huge Laurel and Hardy picture, one of the few objects gracing his new home, with the two Hollywood legends looking particularly downcast. There were further resonances in Stan Laurel – a clown prone to tears from the north of England who had made it bigger than he could have ever imagined. Grinning stand-up comedians didn't loom large in Atkinson's mind. He might compare himself to Barry Humphries in the way he would hide behind characters, but he also told journalist Sheridan Morley that he sees himself as the English Jack Lemmon – 'not that anyone else does as yet'.

By the autumn of 1980 *Not the Nine O'Clock News* was on to its third series and its irreverent posturing had become a British institution. It was notching up an impressive eight million viewers on BBC2 and it had won a Silver Rose at Montreux's annual television awards gala; there was a bestselling book and an album too. But Atkinson was getting itchy, looking for new challenges, such as a West End show. And he still couldn't please his mother, who would call him after a television appearance and say that he looked too thin. He was also talking of writing a sitcom with Richard Curtis along the lines of *Fawlty Towers* meets *Starsky and Hutch*. He revealed to the *Daily Mail* that while he didn't want to analyse his comedy too much, he wasn't actually that happy about his television performances: 'I'm just not at my best on television, working around the clock for sketches which last two minutes at the most; all that whizz, bang, crash stuff. I much prefer the stage where I can stretch myself and really develop

Mr Bean pops up again.

Atkinson plays the piano in his Revue. Plenty of laughs, no piano.

my act.' He felt his current show's sell-by date was approaching and wanted to quit while he was ahead. This was an eminently sensible, if cautious, approach that he would adopt throughout his career.

Success, it seemed, had come too fast, almost too easily. Paradoxically, the ease with which he achieved it was what made him insecure. He couldn't see that it had been easy because he was so uniquely talented; all he could see were the disadvantages and potential pitfalls. He was already gaining a reputation as a perfectionist, but this attention to detail was partly because having risen so fast he didn't want to fall on his face. 'The rate of my success has frightened me,' he said in November 1980. 'I was inundated with offers to do all kinds of jobs, from opening supermarkets to oddball commercials which would have driven me mad.' Worst of all, though, were fans who got too close: 'They tend to scream at me across restaurants: "Give us a funny face, Rowan," which I truly hate.'

He told the *Daily Mail* it had been a shock to his system because it had all been so unplanned: 'I don't recall ever consciously deciding to go into this business. One day it was just a time-consuming hobby, the next day it had become 51 per cent of my life, and suddenly, it was my job.' And his job was very quickly making him part of the showbusiness establishment. In November 1980, Atkinson appeared in front of the Queen at the Royal Variety Performance. A month later he was appointed to the board of directors of the Edinburgh Festival Fringe Society.

Yet not having grown up with a television in the house he hadn't quite realised how established and well known he now was. It was only when he went home for Christmas and was congratulated by countless long-lost family friends appearing at cocktail parties that it dawned on him that he was really famous.

It was an indication of Rowan Atkinson's rapid rise that when he appeared at London's Globe Theatre at the beginning of 1981 it was with a show that wasn't that far removed from his original Hampstead Theatre revue. It also made Atkinson the youngest person ever to have a one-man show in London's West End. It transpired that producer Michael Codron had been trying to get him to mount a show for a lengthy period, but his television success had meant that there simply hadn't been any free time available for a theatrical run.

The humour was the kind of irreverent timeless satire that people had come to expect from Atkinson. His speciality was to poke fun at authority figures; in his headmaster sketch he was still getting his revenge on his old schoolmasters. In his 'Father of the Bride' speech he sent up cringeworthy metaphor-laden wedding speeches, as the proud parent talked about his new in-laws as a 'compost heap' and his new son-in-law as the 'greatest weed growing out of it'.

He also made a mockery of organised religion in a skit in which he played the devil welcoming people to hell: 'Atheists over here please – you must be feeling a right bunch of charlies. And Christians – I'm

afraid the Jews were right.'

His humour often focused on feeling uncomfortable about one's body and the embarrassment of being English and middle class and partially naked in a public place. In one sequence he played a man on a beach trying to put on swimming trunks without removing his trousers. Meanwhile, across the stage, another man wanted to see what was going on but was trying to avoid catching his eye.

In another sketch he impersonated a concert pianist, playing the piano with seemingly elastic hands. His characterisations were so sharp that he hardly required costumes; he simply needed to pucker his lips, bend his pipe-cleaner body with its larger-than-life head and turn into somebody else of a different age or class. For an act about the awkwardness of the human form, on stage at least, he seemed remarkably at ease with his. Not surprisingly *The Times* said he was 'in a league of his own as an entertainer', while celebrities in the audience ranged from Auberon Waugh to David Bowie.

The newly voted Royal Variety Club Showbiz Personality of the Year still had his feet on the ground, mixing his best old material with characters from television – his Ranting Man made an inevitable live appearance to complain about the state of the show mid-way through the set. It wasn't the cutting edge of satire – Pope, Swift and *That Was the Week That Was* didn't need to worry about their reputations – but it was tremendously funny in a jolly silly anti-establishment sort of way. It was more social satire than political satire. A sketch about trying to get served in the post office when you are stuck behind a student wasn't about the run-down state of British post offices or the problems of being a cash-strapped student; it was simply about trying to make oneself heard in a public place. If Atkinson was making a pertinent point it was about the problems of communication. Despite being a deceptive six feet tall he was excellent at playing the little man up against faceless bureaucracy: Norman Wisdom with an M.Sc.

Yet the little man was making it really big. After his success in the 1979 show, he would support Amnesty International in 1981's *The Secret Policeman's Other Ball*. His character comedy was garnering comparisons with the great Peter Sellers; indeed, admitting to a fondness for Inspector Clouseau, prompted rumours that he might take over the role of the accident-prone French detective. And he revealed to the *Guardian* in February 1981 that he was already getting 'Broadway-ish offers'. He wasn't quite sure whether to pursue them yet, though, because he still felt uncomfortable about the cult of celebrity: 'Maybe next year or the year after. The idea interests me, but what frightens me is the celebrity buzz. Over there they tend to pester you a lot.' Which, for Atkinson, would always be much much worse than being ignored.

**Peter Sellers –
another role model.**

The History Man

● ● ● ● ● ● ●

By 1981 Rowan Atkinson had comfortably eased himself into position as Britain's funniest man. His stage work had been acclaimed, his television work had made him famous and quite wealthy. He also had fans in high places. When Prince Charles married Lady Diana Spencer on 29 July, Richard Curtis sent the couple a telegram wishing them 'All love, fun and laughter from the cast and company of the Rowan Atkinson Revue'. A reply promptly followed: 'Enormous thanks for your wonderful message which is heartily reciprocated. Charles and Diana.'

By the autumn of 1981 romance appeared to be on the horizon for the comedian, too, when the *Sun* reported that he was involved with actress Leslie Ash. Like the royal marriage, this relationship too would prove rocky. After a while they separated. Ash married a property developer but then returned to Atkinson and moved in with him, only for things to falter again. But if the path of true love never ran smoothly, his career certainly seemed well oiled. In December 1981 following the three-month run of his show, he was voted Comedy Performer of the Year by the Society of West End Theatres.

With *Not the Nine O'Clock News* about to be consigned to history, due to what he called 'proximity fatigue', however,

40

Atkinson did need some new projects. His sitcom was still bubbling under, but he seemed to be regretting comparing it to *Fawlty Towers*; it was a lot to live up to and now he and Richard Curtis were rethinking it.

In the meantime Rowan occupied himself with smaller, more experimental projects, some of which came to fruition, some of which barely left the drawing board and the tabloid gossip columns. There was a modest film,

Death, directed by Lyndall Hobbs, in which he played a man who has a day to live and is trying to cram in as much as possible. Then there was *Whatever Happened to Bernard Fripp?*, another sideways look at life. Another film diversion was *Summertime*, directed by Bill Forsyth and produced by David Puttnam; this was a story penned by Atkinson about a man on a bicycling holiday in France, which, in terms of setting at least, owed

Showbiz hob-nobbing with Robert Mitchum and Leslie Ash.

41

something to Atkinson's beloved Jacques Tati.

There was also an all-too-brief cameo in Sean Connery's 1983 one-off comeback Bond movie, *Never Say Never Again*. Atkinson played the bumptious Mr Small-Fawcett, the British Consul who has a contretemps with the secret agent. The part was slight, but that was not surprising given that it came about only after Atkinson expressed an interest in being in the film. The producers said it had already been cast, but it was an indication that Rowan Atkinson's commercial clout was growing that for him they changed their minds and commissioned writers Dick Clement and Ian La Frenais to come up with a scene for him – the next day he was on a plane to Nassau to film it. Interestingly Small-Fawcett is the only character Atkinson has ever played who he admits is based on someone in his past – a chap who was at Oxford at the same time as him, whom he recalled having a little Hitler moustache. Everyone else Atkinson has ever played has been a completely fictional creation, albeit with varying degrees of the comic's own personality lurking beneath the mannerisms.

Despite these appearances, he seemed to be slowing down, maybe even losing direction. This wasn't so much a well-planned stage in his career as a mopping-up operation. Atkinson was the most unusual British comedy star to come along in decades, but for a while it looked as if he might be conforming to type and falling into the stardom trap of spending one's way out of a depression. It was already well known that he was a car fanatic,

so news that he had bought a Range Rover was hardly cause to hold the front page. But when it was reported that he was looking for a Scottish castle to buy it did sound as if he was running somewhat off the rails.

In the event the castle didn't materialise, although it had been true that he had put in a bid for a small one. Instead he settled for a Grade II Listed 18th-century rectory in the village of Waterperry in Oxfordshire. It was ideal: a short tootle down the motorway to the BBC in west London, its own tennis courts and plenty of room to park his ever-growing fleet of classic cars. Atkinson confessed that he liked nothing better than to spend his afternoons mowing the lawns. Maybe it was while he was hard at work in his garden thinking about the Scottish castle he nearly bought that he had an idea for a sitcom that could never be compared to *Fawlty Towers* because it was set at a completely different time in British history.

This was the sitcom that Curtis and Atkinson had been working on for ages, but it had undergone a number of rethinks. At one point it was going to be a detective story about bicycle thieves set in Camden Town, with the hero an assistant in a lawyer's office. But both wanted to do something different. It wasn't just the *Fawlty Towers* comparisons that would be invidious, they wanted to be freed from the whole Terry and June style of domestic comedies that were dominating the BBC at the time.

The story of the making of *The Black Adder* is one of the most curious episodes in British sitcom history. In

As the 'Evil King' in his Revue. A chance for a dry run for Edmund Blackadder?

many ways it was a landmark series, not just in terms of the sheer verve and brilliance of the comedy but also in terms of how it nearly didn't come about. The fact that it lasted for four series, despite shaky beginnings, is an object lesson for sitcom makers and critics – never write off something too early.

The funny thing is that the first series (a relative failure compared with later ones), set in a fictional medieval England where Richard III (played by Peter Cook) had actually been rather nice, reputedly came about because of the success of the pilot episode. The BBC was so pleased with the show not made for transmission that in 1983 they lavished a huge budget on the first six parts in which Atkinson played Edmund, Duke of Edinburgh, a snivelling, scheming brother of the heir to the throne of good King Richard IV (Brian Blessed) who takes on the soubriquet of the Black Adder soon after accidentally decapitating Richard III. In fact, they would have been better off shooting it on the cheap in a BBC studio. The budget didn't distract them, but it did place a huge burden of expectations on Atkinson. The idea was to set it at a time when people were mean: 'Humour is about human suffering and hurt. In any humorous situation someone is always having something terrible done to them or rude said about them,' explained the star. It was actually a very good idea for a sitcom. In a way it was sending up all the great BBC costume dramas of the early '70s about Elizabeth I and Henry

VIII. It also paid lip-service to the muck and grime of *Monty Python and the Holy Grail* and recalled the bawdy period humour of Frankie Howerd in *Up Pompeii*. In that sense *The Black Adder* wasn't completely original, but it did take period comedy to even giddier heights.

Instead of filming in a BBC studio as is the norm, the cast travelled up to the Northumbrian coast and filmed in Alnwick Castle. The only trouble was that this quest for authenticity seemed to override the quest for comedy. The wintery shoot was blighted by snowdrifts and things didn't get any

LEFT
A classic sneer from The Black Adder.

A close shave in
The Black Adder.

easier either. It didn't help that the sets were so large, often taking in vast medieval halls, or that there was no room for a studio audience to provide genuine laughter. Even the pudding-basin haircut of Atkinson's character came in for a critical panning. The actor told the *Daily Star* that he would go into shops and people would say 'Poor thing, he's just been let out of the Belgian army.'

With Rik Mayall in Oh What The Hell, **a short film made for John Cleese's Video Arts company.**

The Black Adder, which was first transmitted on 15 June 1983, was not a complete failure, though. Patrick Allen's resonant scene-setting introductions each week obviously made an impression on Vic Reeves and Bob Mortimer, who, nearly a decade later, hired him to do a virtually identical job on their BBC2 series *The Smell of Reeves and Mortimer*. It was also a close-knit affair, linking Atkinson to the new comics just emerging. Rik Mayall had an eyeball-rolling anonymous cameo as Mad Gerald, while Angus Deayton, Atkinson's on-stage straight man, cropped up as a Jumping Jew of Jerusalem, one of the acts booked to entertain the royal court. The series isn't hugely different from the later series, apart from outdoor shots of Atkinson riding a horse or feebly attempting to round up some sheep. Even the crudeness could be explained away as good, honest Chaucerian vulgarity. Perhaps the drubbing was due to the fact that its star had been so successful to date that a backlash was due around now.

Atkinson had his own theory about the negative critical response. In retrospect he thought that maybe Prince Edmund may have been 'a little too dispicable. Heroes of the classically successful British comedy series tend to have won a high degree of sympathy and affection from the British public, like Frank Spencer and even Alf Garnett. Basil Fawlty certainly did. To run a small business and hate your customers is very British.'

In 1986 Atkinson admitted to the *Evening Standard* that he was not very happy about the first series for another reason: 'I think we went to a level of rudeness which surprised even me. I don't mind rude humour as long as it is funny, but there is nothing worse than a rude joke that doesn't work.'

With Ben Elton: the two first worked together on Blackadder II **and their partnership continues today.**

He may have been thinking at the time about his codpiece shaped like an erect penis, but there were also plenty of other examples of medieval rudery to choose from.

The Black Adder was Atkinson's first real failure. Not even an Emmy in America – the television equivalent of an Oscar – could sweeten the pill. It wasn't a complete disaster, but after high expectations it was a huge disappointment. The team of Atkinson, Curtis and Goodall was relieved, however, that they were told there would be a second series. Even if others were less confident, they realised that with some nipping, tucking and rethinking a second series would put things right. With everyone apart from sidekicks Baldrick (Tony Robinson) and Lord

Percy (Tim McInnerney) dying at the end of the series after being poisoned, the creators would have to have a good idea to bring the cast back.

The main change for the second series, which was screened in 1985, was to set the action a century on in the court of Queen Elizabeth (Miranda Richardson) so that the cast could play the descendants of the original ensemble. The other change was the replacement of Atkinson and William Shakespeare on the writing team with Ben Elton, the fiery young alternative comic who had made his name as a co-writer on *The Young Ones*.

Elton was, in many ways, a complete mirror image of Atkinson in terms of personality and ambition. Atkinson had sort of stumbled into a comedy career and felt it could end at any time, and it wouldn't be the end of the world if it did. In fact it was only with *The Black Adder* that he finally changed his occupation on his passport: 'I tried to maintain engineer as a career for as long as possible,' he joked to the *Daily Star*, 'mainly for insurance purposes. You have no idea of the quantum leap in the premium when I made the change.' Elton, on the other hand, had set his heart on an artistic life from an early age. At Manchester University he toiled away in the drama department writing plays and performing them at any opportunity. His friendship with Rik Mayall and Adrian Edmondson had helped his career and he was now hot property as a writer and a constantly improving stand-up comedian. The two had contrasting talents too. Atkinson's skills and ideas were often physical; Elton, like Curtis, was a lover of words. For the next three series the emphasis was decidedly on the linguistic side, producing not so much situation comedy as situation tragedy.

The second series nearly didn't happen. Just before it went ahead the team received a bolt from the blue from new BBC boss Michael Grade. He had been looking over the accounts and had decided that in the first series there were not enough laughs per pound. The joke doing the rounds at the BBC at the time was that the first

Making history fun the Atkinson way.

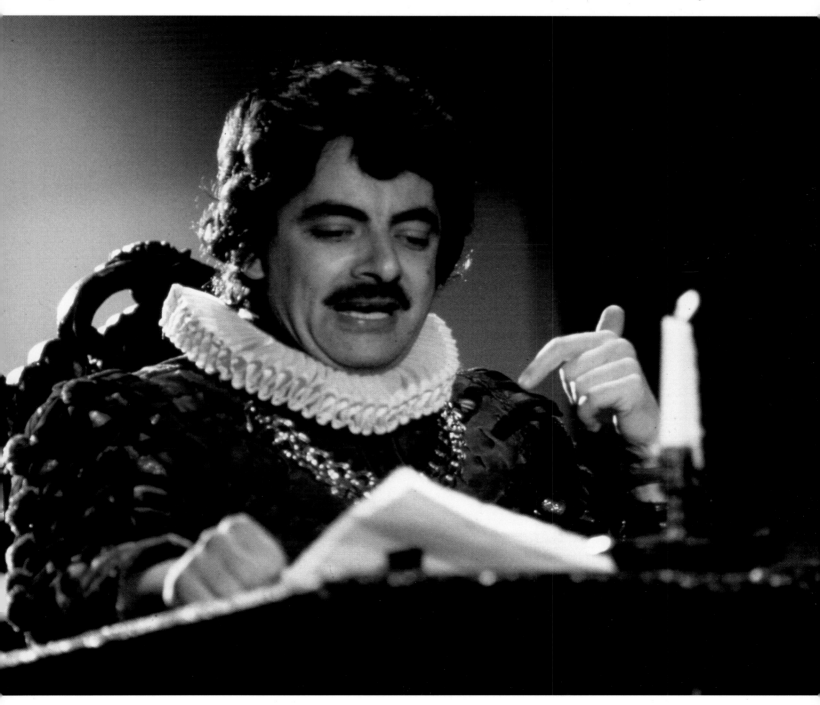

to cheat, sneaking peeks in any way he could at his neighbour's papers. Other sketches homed in on the problems of communication, with varying degrees of decency and taste. There was a skit about three deaf, dumb and blind men run down by a combine harvester; a song from One-Eyed Jim, the country singer who plays guitar back to front; and news for the hard of hearing using increasingly absurd sign language instead of subtitles. There was a new Atkinson creeping in, but the old one had yet to creep out completely. He was still excorcising the ghosts of St Bees in the sketch in which a strict disciplinarian headmaster apologises for beating a boy to death, while that malleable body was used to great effect in a scene in which a passenger on the London Underground is pestered by an invisible man. If some of the sketches seemed a trifle down-market at times, he was unashamed, he said in the press, even though they might have seemed odd, coming from someone of such cultured stock: 'I'm very aware of being a member of the educated middle class and that some-times my comedy is aimed at them. But I also like the simpler, less preten-tious stuff that appeals much further down the market, like *Blackadder II*.'

The success of his West End shows brought some of the old confidence back. He made some rare public appearances with his new girlfriend, BBC make-up artist Sunetra Sastry, and he was prepared to make his opin-ions known on issues outside comedy, speaking out against violence on tele-vision and saying that he preferred to watch *Songs of Praise*.

In October 1986 Rowan Atkinson made his Broadway début, appropri-ately at the Atkinson Theater, with *Rowan Atkinson at the Atkinson*. If this was the big test of whether his comedy was international, he certainly failed it. But then again, his failure might

With his wife, Sunetra, attend-ing a party as characters from The Addams Family.

**Another show,
another vicar ...**

have as much to do with the attitudes and status of the American critics as with the fundamental Britishness of Rowan Atkinson. The show closed after 14 performances – eight previews and six shows. The closure, which lost backers a reported £500,000, was largely put down to the review of Frank Rich in the *New York Times*. Not for nothing is he called 'the Butcher of Broadway'. In a scathing attack on Atkinson, Rich concluded that 'the melding of English and American cultures is not yet complete.'

The star, clearly shaken by the venom of the press, called Rich a feudal king with too much power and responded in the *Daily Mail*: 'The only way I'll go back is if I can take out insurance against that man coming anywhere near me.' Calming down a little, he looked on the bright side, calling it a 'disgracefully vicious and irrational attack. The only good thing to come out of the whole venture is that now I will be home for Christmas.' There was a certain amount of relief that it was all over. 'It was like the maths teacher not turning up – thank God I can do something else now. I'm off the hook.' Rich's review wasn't simply an assault on the star; it was a critique of a lavatorial vein of British humour that has been around since Chaucer:

'As long as the British public maintains its fondness for toilet humor there will always be an England. Mr Atkinson is very big on toilet jokes and he is very big in England ... It's not inconceivable that this comic's biggest fans at home are products of an upbringing that encourages boys to tame their nasty bowel habits at an early age, with the consequences that their obsession with alimentary by-products persists right through Oxford and Cambridge.'

Atkinson, for so long a performer with few allies in show business, suddenly found some unlikely supporters in the press. Bob Monkhouse sprang to his defence conceding that 'New York is a tough place. The RSC once did *Julius Caesar* there. When Caesar was stabbed on stage half the audience left because they didn't want to get involved.'

Rich's review found little positive in the show, even finding fault with the moments he found funny: 'The director has done his star no favors by letting the poor sketches and even the occasional decent one (the contortions of a narcoleptic church worshiper) drag on well past their breaking points. Were *Rowan Atkinson at the Atkinson* to be edited down to its wittiest jokes however, even its title might have to go.'

Producer Arthur Cantor called Rich's piece 'not a review, a train crash' and pointed to other reviews that had been much more favourable. Clive Barnes in the *New York Post*, for instance, had called it 'very funny, hilarious and sidesplitting', which makes you wonder if Barnes and Rich had been at the same show. *Newsday* called Atkinson a very droll fellow and even went on to say that he 'brings us a brand of British humor that travels well'.

Maybe the problems were more political than personal. There was a certain amount of hubris in store for Atkinson the moment he was booked for a show

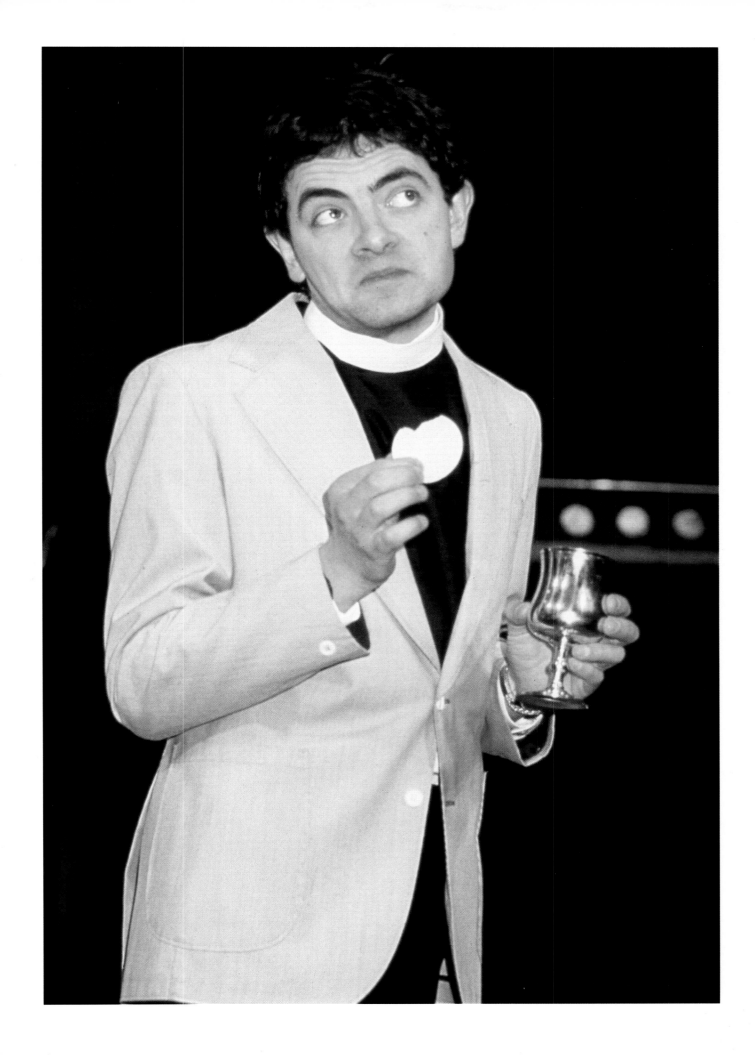

A dramatic departure: Atkinson tackles Chekhov and co-star Cheryl Campbell in The Sneeze.

right on Broadway. Even a well-known American star might have had difficulty shifting tickets at $50 a time, so perhaps it was no surprise that the shows for this unknown Limey were thinly attended even before the *New York Times* review. Experts said that he should have started off-Broadway and built up a word-of-mouth following. Certainly that was the way Eddie Izzard made a respectable dent in the Big Apple a decade later. Lenny Henry was even more cautious than that, preferring to turn up in clubs and try his luck as an unknown. Then again, very few English comedy stars had made a big impression on the American stage since *Beyond the Fringe* in the '60s. Maybe Atkinson made the grave mistake of thinking that the Americans would share his reference points of housemasters, vicars and BBC news-readers, or at least understand them. He would make a bigger impression on America when in 1989 he appeared in a modest low-budget black-and-white film short with American comic Steven Wright entitled *The Appointments of Dennis Jennings*, in which he played a psychiatrist and Wright played his patient. But with his live show the critics couldn't see further than the bottom jokes and they were not too keen on those.

There was still an abiding sense in which Atkinson felt like an outsider. This man out of time was too small-'c' conservative for the post-punk anarchy of the alternative comedy scene; and in a world where the word was paramount he was still an unusually body-conscious physical entertainer. While

he shied away from being known only as the Funny Face Man, he did feel that his talents would have been better appreciated in a previous age. In September 1986 he explained his predicament to the *Mail on Sunday*: 'If I had been a contemporary of Charlie Chaplin I feel I might have been able to exploit myself to the full. I am a visual animal.'

After the questionable reviews for *The Nerd* and the downright critical mauling on Broadway, he was still keen to prove himself on stage in the flesh. While television was fine, there had always been something special about a live appearance. Atkinson's humour was often about the culture of embarrassment and the phenomenon of deflated expectations, and there was an added thrill when the audience was there in person to share in the artist's emotional ups and downs.

He cast around for new challenges. What could be more emotional than Chekhov? Atkinson's next project was to appear in a collection of short playlets by the seminal playwright under the umbrella title of *The Sneeze*; some were original, some were adapted by writer Michael Frayn. It seemed on the surface like a huge departure, but the star, who was taking on a heavy responsibility, appearing in seven of the eight shorts, didn't think it was that much of a digression. *The Bear*, for instance, he described as 'gripping, tragic and terribly funny, with a humour more sadistic than *Blackadder*'. In the plays, which were previewed at the Bradford Alhambra and Newcastle Theatre Royal before coming to London in

September 1988, Atkinson teamed up with two eminent actors: Timothy West,
who had played so many historical characters in his time, ranging from Edward
VII to Churchill, that it was a surprise that he had never appeared in
Blackadder; and Cheryl Campbell, best known to television viewers as the

errant schoolteacher in Dennis Potter's *Pennies From Heaven*.

Once again, Atkinson was taking a different route to that of his comic contemporaries. There was nothing unusual about a comedian doing drama – everyone from Stanley Holloway to Alexei Sayle had done their bit of the Bard – but the tendency was for funny men to play uncomplicated funny characters such as Bottom, Touchstone or the Fool. This move only emphasised Atkinson's claims that he wasn't from a stand-up comedy tradition. There was nothing wrong with comedy, but he simply wasn't a gag merchant. To him *The Sneeze* was his chosen way of 'being serious without being serious'. It seemed a natural means of gaining some more theatrical credibility without completely deserting his comedy fan base: a way for the perennial face-puller to stretch himself further. As for the possibility of playing some Shakespearean comedy, Atkinson explained in the London *Evening Standard* why he had avoided that path, although he had considered it: 'We even thought of Shakespeare but the parts have been played so often the audience spends the whole evening making comparisons.' Besides, for a performer who specialised in losers, there was plenty of comic mileage to be gleaned from *The Sneeze*, as most of the characters he played in it were, he said, 'miserable downtrodden men'. The plays were also a way of pleasing his mother. She had been embarrassed by the rudeness of *Blackadder* and her son pointed out to the press that she hadn't enjoyed his performances in a

play since he was Mephistopheles as a schoolboy.

Because the Chekhov playlets were short they were more of a bridge between full-blown dramas and sketches, and they gave Atkinson the chance to demonstrate a wide range of mimetic and thespian skills. In *Drama*

LEFT
Trying to distract Timothy West in The Sneeze.

Wigging out in The Sneeze.

The comedy nuns routine with Jeff Goldblum in The Tall Guy.

he played a writer being rude to a prospective rival; *The Sneeze* was a wordless three-hander. *The Proposal* was all wigs and hypochondria, while *The Evils of Tobacco* was a pure Chekhovian monologue, mixing comedy and tragedy. Atkinson described it as the most serious piece of acting he had ever done, saying 'the laugh freezes on your lips'. *The Bear*, however, rammed home the predicament for the eternal clown: Atkinson was supposed to be playing it straight but according to some reviews he managed to upstage West and Campbell with a seemingly unintentional funny walk as he left the stage.

Until this stage, there had not been a lot of scandal in Atkinson's career. His job was to appear on the stage and screen to make people laugh. Despite his claims that he was a standard-issue lonely comic, there was little in his private life to suggest a truly dark side. If there was anything venal, ruthless or tyrannical he had kept it well hidden. In his casual clothes he was almost like the Cliff Richard of Comedy – your daughters would be safe with him. His press persona seemed to play up to this with quotes such as 'People think because I can make them laugh on the stage, I'll be able to make them laugh in person. That isn't the case at all. I am essentially a rather quiet, dull person who just happens to be a performer.' But maybe there was something there after all. When he started filming his next movie, it seemed as if he was admitting to the world that he wasn't such a squeaky clean character after all.

As alter ego Ron Anderson, alongside Emma Thompson in The Tall Guy.

The Tall Guy was something of an old pals act. Mel Smith was the director, and Richard Curtis wrote it. In the film, American actor Jeff Goldblum plays a struggling performer who gets a job as the sidekick of a comedian Ron Anderson, played by Rowan Atkinson. The character is mean and nasty to Goldblum, or, as Atkinson put it, 'a complete and utter shitbag'. Inevitably the film seemed to be about Atkinson himself: its original title was *Camden Town Boy* – both Atkinson and Curtis had lived in that north London district – and

Goldblum's role could easily be compared to that of Angus Deayton's job in Atkinson's live show: Atkinson had admitted that he was a stickler for discipline. And just to ram the point home, both the fictional and real entertainers shared the initials 'R.A.' Not surprisingly, Atkinson made a pre-emptive strike before people assumed the sadism and cruelty was all true. He admitted in the press that it had elements of truth in it but pointed out that he hoped 'people will realise my part is grossly exaggerated.' When *The Tall Guy* finally opened in April 1989, Atkinson explained where his motivation for playing someone who liked humiliating people came from – even if he wasn't like that himself: 'You only have to go through a fairly mild public-school education to have witnessed cruelty. If you tried to do what I did, which was to establish your individuality, you become a loner and to some extent I experienced bullying and cruelty. I am really a meek person and keen to please, so I grew up terribly conscious of cruelty. Comedy may well be my way of taking revenge all these years later.' It wasn't clear whether he was talking about Rowan Atkinson or Ron Anderson, but given the fact that he sounded as if he was describing his own background the inevitable conclusion was that they had more things in common than he cared to admit.

By 1987, Atkinson was exorcising the demons of his Broadway nightmare with more live work, but it was not without its mishaps. He appeared at Montreal's Just For Laughs Festival in July and was going down a storm until his microphone cut out and he was unable to continue. In the autumn he went off on a tour of Australia, where his television programmes – *Blackadder* was an Australian co-production – had already made him famous.

As the failed American invasion receded into the distance the effect was less shattering. In a way Frank Rich's review was so vituperative and isolated that Atkinson took it less to heart in retrospect. Rich was so dismissive that he couldn't find a constructive thing to say about a show that in various forms under different titles had been a success elsewhere in the English-speaking world. It was as if he had got out of bed on the wrong side that morning and would have harangued the star for the colour of the loo paper in the theatre's toilets if everything else had been to his liking. Life had to go on and in the next decade Atkinson would have the last laugh, going down a storm in America.

By the late '80s Atkinson was more popular than ever. After the doubts about making a second series of *Blackadder*, there was never any debate about whether there would be a third series. The only question was when it would be set. The team provided the answer in 1987, moving the action to 1790 and the court of the Prince Regent. Atkinson was the port-swilling butler to the Prince Regent, played with exceptional dimness by Hugh Laurie.

Now that the characters and the concept had bedded in, writers Elton and Curtis had more fun than ever playing with historical characters and events of the day. There is a disaster when the only copy of Dr Johnson's dictionary is tossed on to the fire and much hilarity when *Blackadder* asks Baldrick to bring him some meat between two slices of bread. 'Like Gerald Lord Sandwich had the other night?' asks his faithful retainer. 'That's right, a round of Geralds.'

If the series was very funny when it hit the screens, interviews with the star suggested that it was less amusing off camera, as the supporting cast became more and more concerned about their roles. Tim McInnerney had reportedly even pulled out for fear of being typecast as a twit, though after a break he would return, more twittish than ever, for the fourth and final series.

An interview in the *Daily Mirror* hinted at backstage difficulties when Atkinson said it was amazing that the programme ever gets made because 'we're dreadful. It's very democratic because everyone gets involved, but we tear every line apart and discuss each ridiculous little detail of the programme.' Even with writers of the calibre of Curtis and Elton, getting everyone happy with their lines was a painstaking process, but despite the friction, Atkinson still had the full support of Tony Robinson, who, even when he wasn't in character as the stupidly loyal Baldrick, called Atkinson 'the finest clown of his generation'.

Even though he was a stickler for discipline in his professional life, Atkinson did overstep the mark while on the road. In July 1988 he pleaded guilty at Newbury Magistrates Court to driving at 114 m.p.h on the M4 in his Aston Martin Zagato; he was disqualified for two weeks and fined £150. In the end the ban wasn't too onerous; although it was hard for Atkinson to cope without being able to drive his beloved cars, he was in America for part of the fortnight. The only real pain came from deciding to sell his car to help him to avoid speeding again. On *Desert Island Discs* he had told Sue Lawley that he would like his luxury to be his electric-blue Aston Martin. A nice touch was that he also wanted a tin of wax polish so that he could keep it in pristine condition.

By 1989 Rowan Atkinson had been in show business for little more than ten years, but he had done just about everything apart from star in his own Hollywood action blockbuster – although he would soon find the time to chip in to Nicolas Roeg's *The Witches*, playing a grumpy hotel clerk to Anjelica Huston's vampish lead role. He had television success, stage success and a reasonable amount of respect for his straight excursions. His work rate was as prodigious as his hit rate. Something had to give and it seemed to be his stomach. In January the *Sun* reported that he was suffering from an ulcer due to overwork. This intimation of his mortality didn't exactly make Atkinson take a break, but maybe it did make him take stock. The end of the decade would mark the end of one great television character and the emergence of another.

Bean in a Mustang in California.

Caught in the Crossfire

● ● ● ● ● ● ● ● ● ●

B y the late '80s British television was involved in a fierce ratings war. While the soaps battled it out to see who could come up with the most compelling storylines to grab the viewers, when it came to comedy, the network chiefs had a different tactic. Rather than develop new talent and new ideas they simply waved their chequebooks and signed up the most successful acts from the other side. There was nothing intrinsically new about this – Morecambe and Wise had swapped sides back in the '70s – but with satellite becoming more popular, video sales to think of and advertising revenue constantly growing, there was more than ever at stake. The ITV companies also had to keep the quality of their programming up so that their franchises would be safe when the Conservative government allowed prospective new networks to pitch for them.

In the middle of this competitive market, Britian's top comedy stars would change channels as skilled footballers changed clubs. Channel 4's Vic Reeves and Bob Mortimer would soon go to the BBC, and the *Comic Strip* team would make the same journey. The commercial chiefs needed to hit back

and Rowan Atkinson was the perfect target. He may not have been as hip as the *Comic Strip* but he had huge commercial clout and appealed to viewers of all ages. And of course his first television outing, *Canned Laughter*, had been on ITV. In May 1989 it was announced that Rowan Atkinson had

Fun in the foliage: Blackadder Goes Forth.

signed a reported £250,000 deal with Thames Television to make two hour-long specials. It wasn't clear what they would be, but it seemed to signal the imminent demise of *Blackadder.*

It wasn't an inspired choice, but it did make perfect sense. Thames certainly had a good record with visual comedy, having had huge international success with Benny Hill; but with the advent of political correctness Hill and his dolly birds were out of favour, and the company needed a new, younger comic to replace him. Atkinson would fit the bill and even make Hill's global slapstick success seem modest.

Meanwhile back at the BBC *Blackadder* wasn't going to go down without a bang. The ratings war would seem like a tea party compared with the war during which the final *Blackadder* would be set. In September 1989 the fourth series, *Blackadder Goes Forth*, was launched. This time round the action was focused on the fighting on the Western Front in 1917. Atkinson played Captain Edmund Blackadder, the careworn moustachioed descendant of his previous incarnations; Tony Robinson was back as his faithful batman, Private Baldrick. After dim, dashing and devious incarnations, Edmund Blackadder was simply deadpan, the victim of a humour bypass but prone to the longest one-liners in sitcom history. Atkinson's monstrous creation sent up his own comic hero Charlie Chaplin in an episode where he describes him as being about as funny as getting an arrow in your head and then finding a gas bill attached to it. In Blackadder's opinion Baldrick

proved himself to be the only person even less funny than Chaplin by trying to impersonate him using a dead slug as a moustache.

The series that had started five years earlier with Peter Cook being accidently decapitated at the Battle of Bosworth by the Beeb's anti-hero had a more violent backdrop to it than ever. Inevitably there were complaints on taste grounds about setting a sitcom during the First World War (although the Second World War never seemed to harm *Dad's Army*), but the team's equally inevitable reply was that nothing in the series was as absurd as some of the events that really happened, such as messenger pigeons being tried for treason and soldiers being shot by their own side for refusing to wear helmets. As viewers were to find out in the poignant final episode, the series was hardly celebrating war but wholeheartedly and explicitly condemning the mass slaughter of men whom the officers in command considered to be little more than cannon fodder. If Atkinson had never been particularly political before, with the help of the committed radical Ben Elton he certainly was here. Lines about the war being over by Christmas, the only trouble being that no one knew which Christmas had a convincing ring to them; these men have been fighting for so long they have forgotten what they were fighting about. At times *Blackadder Goes Forth* could have been a documentary, not merely a situation comedy.

The success of the series was clearly down to the smallest details being honed to perfection. In the script rooms debates raged over whether 'small sausage' was funnier than 'middle-sized sausage', whether the word 'Congo' was fundamentally more amusing than 'Tanganyika'. Gallows humour was the main motif. In the episode entitled 'Corporal Punishment', Blackadder is sentenced to death for shooting – and eating – the pigeon carrying his orders to attack the enemy. The writers even included a nod to *Dad's Army* by naming two of the firing squad Corporal Jones and Private Fraser. There were plenty of in-jokes for loyal followers since the early days of *Blackadder*. Miranda Richardson cropped up again as Blackadder's love interest Nurse Mary Fletcher-Brown in 'General Hospital'; while in 'Major Star'; Gabrielle Glaister played Bob, the soldier who is patently female. In the second series, she had played Kate, who disguises herself as a boy called Bob and is about to marry Blackadder when she is whisked away by Lord Flashheart (whose swashbuckling descendant Squadron Leader Lord Flashheart also appeared in the fourth series, played once again by the scene-stealing Rik Mayall). If you wanted to dig deeper, the idea for the cross-dressing may have come from Atkinson's awareness of the origins of his own middle name: Sebastian in Shakespeare's *Twelfth Night* becomes embroiled in a case of mistaken identity when his sister Viola dresses up as him.

The regular supporting cast was more impressive than ever, with much of the line-up made up of performers who were now stars in their own right. Stephen Fry was back as General Sir

Anthony Cecil Hogmanay Melchett; Hugh Laurie was in chinless dullard mode once more as Lieutenant the Hon George Colthurst St Barleigh; Tim McInnerney returned after a break as Captain Kevin Darling. Conditions are filthy, the commanders are sadistic, after three years the men have advanced as far as an asthmatic ant carrying heavy shopping, and Baldrick is doing the cooking.

With Fry and Laurie both coming from Cambridge, *Blackadder Goes Forth* might go down as the most

During the filming of Blackadder Goes Forth.

77

The cream of the modern comedy crop: Dawn French, Atkinson, Hugh Laurie, Stephen Fry.

middle-class sitcom ever broadcast. Certainly, Fry, Laurie and Atkinson had all had similar comfortable middle-class backgrounds. Fry in fact would be Atkinson's best man when he married Sunetra Sastry in New York in February 1990. Atkinson and Sastry had been together for a while now, but one contemporary's recollection of

their first date seemed to typify Atkinson's British reserve off screen combined with Mr Bean's pratfalls on it. Legend has it that he invited her out to dinner and didn't say anything for 15 minutes. He then asked her to pass the ketchup. Then he disappeared into the toilets when his zip broke and he needed to find a safety

pin. If this isolated incident provided one picture of Atkinson off-duty as a composite of his comic creations, Stephen Fry offered what is probably the most accurate assessment of Atkinson's complex character to date when he said in *The Observer* that 'Rowan has not an ounce of showbiz in him. It is as if God had an extra jar of comic talent and for a joke gave it to a nerdy, anoraked northern chemist.' Another friend perhaps came almost as close to pinning down Atkinson by revealing that 'he likes nothing better than to be under the lawnmower draining the sump.'

With his announcement that *Blackadder Goes Forth* would be the final series Atkinson tacitly acknowledged that there were more problems off screen than were apparent on screen. In the *Sun* he said; 'I think we have gone as far as we can go with it. It's a shame because the audience was enjoying it most when we were enjoying making it the least. It's like selling a car – the best time to sell is also the best time to keep it.' In the *Daily Mirror* he admitted that conflict over lines had been about more than just whether 'Congo' was funnier than 'Tanganyika'. 'Whereas perhaps it used to be just me who wanted his script discussed, suddenly everyone wants a major discussion on all their lines.' It was as if everyone had inherited Atkinson's perfection disease and all of them were terrified of failure. It made the production process fraught but it also produced one of the BBC's all-time favourite sitcoms.

Each series of *Blackadder* had ended with the cast dead, but while previous instalments had been little more than cartoon killings, the final scene in the final episode, transmitted on 2 November 1989, was much more than black comedy. Melchett has ordered his men over the top and after much prevarication it seems that they have no choice. No plan, however cunning, can save them now. An unusually dignified Captain Blackadder leads his loyal men over the top to certain death and the screen fills with poppies.

Once audiences had got over the most moving scene in the history of sitcom, they would be left with memories of a classic series, but also tantalising glimpses of what might have been if *Blackadder* had continued. There was a 1988 Dickensian Christmas special in which *Blackadder* became Scrooge, which could have easily become a series; then there was a Comic Relief sketch in which *Blackadder* was set in a space-age future. While there was a rich vein of comedy to be mined there, comparisons with BBC2's *Red Dwarf* would have been inevitable. Then there was a rumour that *Blackadder* would come back as a '60s rock group with Tony Robinson playing a drummer called Bald Rick, but it was not to be.

It was revealed in *Melody Maker* that there had been talk of making *Blackadder* an evil Tory MP until ITV launched *The New Statesman* with Rik Mayall, and Curtis and Co. thought that there was too much overlap. Rumours flew about in the tabloids that this had caused a rift between Mayall and Atkinson, but there was little sign of it when the *Comic Strip* icon cameoed in the episode 'Private

Plane' as a swashbuckling, womanising, jodhpur-slapping pilot called Lord Flashheart, a rakish descendant of the groin-thrusting blonde-locked Flashheart who steals Blackadder's bride-to-be, Bob, away from him in *Blackadder II*.

While his fans waited to see what Atkinson would do on ITV, they would have got a shock when the first fruits of Atkinson's lucrative deal appeared. This wasn't a comedy at all, but it was a chance for Atkinson to reveal to the nation his passion for fast cars. In *The Driven Man* he waxed lyrical about his

motor-mania. In the mid '80s he had been buying and selling cars like there was no tomorrow. It wasn't necessarily an investment, he was more interested in the mechanics of different machines than the potential profits. He had bought an unusual Mercedes because he was fascinated by the hydraulic system, but having driven 50 yards in it he realised it wasn't the car for him and he sold it after just three weeks.

Cars seemed to be his way of escaping from not just comedy but also the outside world. They were a movable

LEFT
Tragic hero Captain Edmund Blackadder.

With Ben Elton, writer and friend, through thick and Thin Blue Line.

but personal space – he could use them as a thick carapace as he negotiated the modern media and all its complications and intrusions. At times it really seemed as if he preferred cars to people. Even a decade after the event he told *Today* that one of his strongest memories was of passing his HGV test: 'The thrill of making 2,000 people in a theatre laugh is but a light breeze compared to the tornado of excitement that I felt at that moment.'

Filming Bean **and creating mayhem**.

As a new decade dawned it was time for Rowan Atkinson to unveil his latest creation. On New Year's Day 1990 the first 30-minute Mr Bean adventure was screened on ITV, attracting a staggering audience of 13 million. If *Blackadder* was a Volkswagen Golf, an acquired taste but solid, reliable, a little daring and always popular, *Mr Bean* was a Ford Escort, lighter, less demanding, inclined to play safe but instantly a huge hit. For many viewers this bumbling mostly silent cross between Charlie Chaplin and Frank Spencer was a new sight. People who had followed Rowan Atkinson's career since the late '70s, however, would have experienced more than a hint of *déjà vu*. Atkinson himself was happy to admit that Mr Bean was an extension of some of the sketches he had been performing live ever since Oxford. There were precursors of Bean in *Canned Laughter*, which had gone out on ITV over a decade earlier. The irony was that there was an industry rumour that he had earlier offered *Bean* to the Beeb and Auntie had turned it down. It was no secret that he, Richard Curtis and new writer

RIGHT

Atkinson making comedy seem like a piece of cake.

Atkinson and BAFTA – one of many awards he collected in the '80s.

Robin Driscoll used old sketches as a basis for *Bean*; they would watch Atkinson's old stage-show routines and see if these could be adapted for the box. Physical sketches such as the man trying to change into his swimming trunks before he pulled his trousers down formed the basis of Bean's struggles with the 20th century. Atkinson had been accused of being an alien at school, now he took this a stage further – each programme started with Bean being beamed down to earth, an other-worldly idiot savant with leather patches on his sleeves. Trying to help people out, he is a Heath Robinson cartoon come to life who invariably creates havoc, causes misery and provokes embarrassment. It seemed a very English form of embarrassment, but it would prove to be Atkinson's most successful character internationally, confirming that no single nationality has a monopoly on morons. In meetings the team would invoke the mantra 'think of the Egyptians'. The absence of language meant borders were immaterial: or maybe the rest of the world just liked to see the stereotypical dim-witted, awkward Englishman in action – all that was missing was the bowler hat.

It was clear from the moment *Mr Bean* went out that it would be a major mainstream success. Audience research showed that the viewers ranged in age from four to a hundred years old. People called Bean started writing to the programme saying that their name was now the cause of great embarrassment. It could have been so different, though. In the debate over what to call this nameless character

that had been around for years, Atkinson considered Mr White, then, rejecting colours, experimented with the sounds of different vegetables before coming up with Bean. It might have been people called Mr Cauliflower or Mr Cabbage who would have had to live down an association with this clumsy everyman.

Bean never came naturally to Atkinson, but there was an instinctive element to him, which arose from the fact that he was so similar to Atkinson the inquisitive boy. The performer admitted in interviews that a lot of Bean was him as a nine-year-old, which he had also said about the Nerd:

'I know him better than any other character I've done. I prefer to look round the back of things rather than take them at face value. Bean, too, is someone who, presented with an advertising hoarding, won't just read it and walk on; he'll always want to go round the back, look at the structure of the sign, wonder how it is put together, pull out a bolt and "whoops".'

Bean's silent visual antics suggested that Rowan Atkinson wasn't quite as reluctant to resort to face-pulling as he had been in the late '80s. He seemed confident enough to return to his roots and he had good reason to feel confident. With *Blackadder* still fresh in people's minds and *Mr Bean* making waves, 1990 was Atkinson's *annus mirabilis* in terms of awards. In March he picked up a BAFTA for Best Light Entertainment Performer, while *Blackadder* was named Best Comedy Show of the Year. He was also voted BBC Personality of the Year. Not surprisingly the BBC began to re-run all

Ending the decade on a high: Atkinson flanked by Sunetra and his BBC TV Personality Award 1989.

RIGHT

Bearded and brooding.

four series, while foreign sales were astonishing, with the series being sold in places as unlikely as Iceland and Hong Kong. *Mr Bean* was also making its mark, picking up the coveted Golden Rose at Montreux as well as the press award and the city award. There were already plans afoot to make more, but Atkinson wanted to do them as occasional one-offs to keep them special, resisting the opportunity to cash in with a series straight away. As ever he seemed to be playing his cards close to his chest. Even Howard Goodall, who had known Atkinson since Oxford, said after the Montreux win that 'Nobody knows what goes on inside the inner recesses.' Even the instant success of *Bean* couldn't stop Atkinson's angst from resurfacing. Whereas *Blackadder* had taken its time winning awards he felt that *Bean* had been a hit too quickly and there would now be pressure to continue the winning formula.

Part of the success of *Mr Bean* was due to the fact that behind the scenes there was an experienced team with an impeccable track record in television comedy. Director John Howard Davies had worked with Atkinson on *Not the Nine O'Clock News* and by now knew how he ticked: 'He is a very methodical performer. His instincts are great, but he also has an intellectual approach to his stuff that television can accommodate well. I think he's still an electrical engineer at heart – he likes to know how the comic circuitry works.'

Atkinson's interest in the machinery of the industry meant that it was no surprise when he decided to set up his own production company. This way he wouldn't just make more money by being the producer of his shows; he would also be able to retain more creative control. One of his few relative failures had been appearing in *The Nerd*, a project that he didn't produce and subsequently had very little control over.

The other attraction of running one's own company was the ability to kick-start projects. One of the few glitches in his career had been the faltering film appearances. He said in the press that he was getting fed up with being offered endless film roles that had been turned down by Dudley Moore and John Cleese: 'villains, butlers and freaks'. With his own production company he would be able to cut out the middle man and develop his own projects.

By 1991 continued success meant a hectic schedule. In the spring he followed his mentor John Cleese and

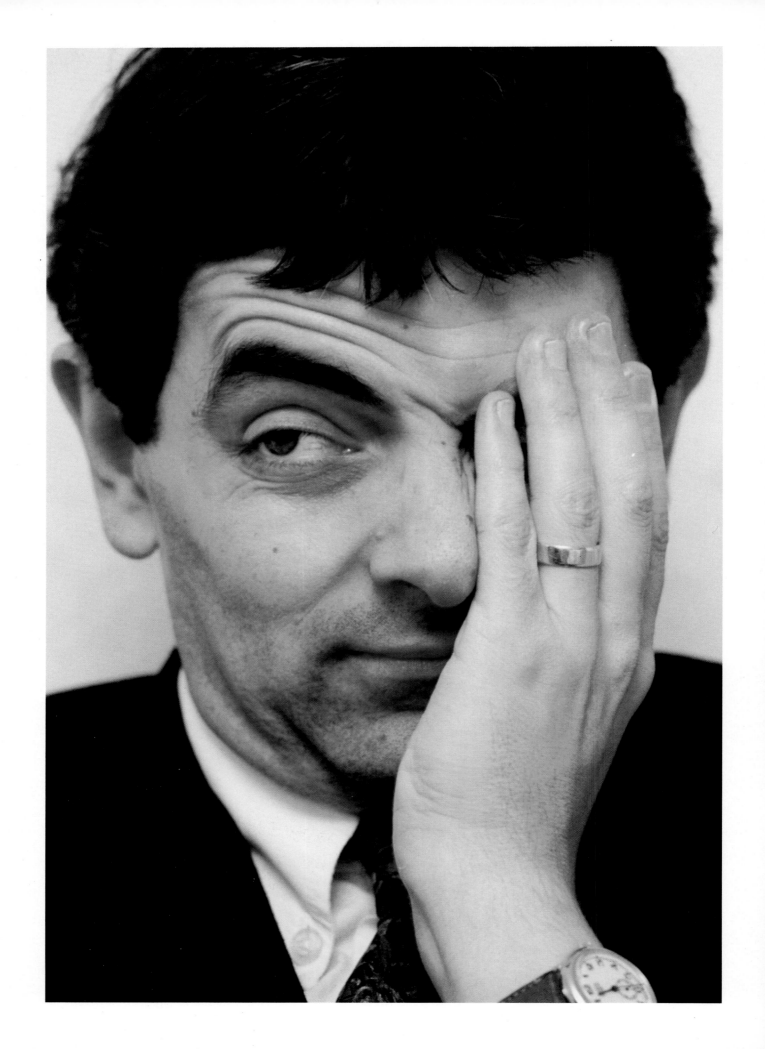

appeared in a cameo in the American sitcom *Cheers* as a barman, suggesting that despite his Broadway flop there was growing interest in his work over there. *Blackadder* was a cult show on cable and there were rumours that he had turned down a $70-million television deal with one of the American television networks.

It was success and breaking new ground rather than money that motivated Atkinson, but that didn't stop him from finally succumbing to the lucrative lure of making adverts. In the early '80s he had briefly had a stint advertising the *Guardian*, but unlike younger comedians such as Harry Enfield he had resisted doing ads for fear that it would dent his credibility. In 1991, however, he did agree to promote Barclaycard for a reported £750,000, which, along with around 15 per cent in royalties for the sale of *Blackadder* videos, would enable him to buy a Kensington town house without selling his Oxfordshire rectory. He seemed fairly unashamed about his earnings, saying in the *Daily Mirror*, 'I uphold the new middle-class tradition of only being funny for financial gain – as opposed to working-class comics who were funny all the time.'

These ads were different to the run-of-the-mill comedians-cashing-in-on-their-fame, though. They were directed by Atkinson's old *Not the Nine O'Clock News* producer John Lloyd and worked as pocket-sized comedy sketches. Atkinson's character in the credit card promos was another great bumbler, self-styled super-spy Richard Latham. In each ad he appears to be teaching his young acolyte Bough,

played by Henry Naylor, how to be a secret agent. And in each ad he is hoist by his own petard, falling foul of his methods while Bough with his Barclaycard come up trumps. Atkinson treated the job as if it were another television series, which in effect it was. 'He loves to get into a role and know how his character would react in every situation. That made working with him more challenging,' said the ad agency copywriter Jon Matthews in the *TV Times*.

In the first ad the duo are in Egypt and while Latham buys an ancient rug for cash in the local market, Bough explains that one of the benefits of Barclaycard is protection if goods are damaged. Latham suggests that little can go wrong on the banks of the Nile, but little does he know that as he speaks the other end of his rug has caught alight on an oil lamp and as he walks away his investment is going up in flames.

According to Jon Matthews, Atkinson agreed to do it only if it was a departure from previous television characters: 'Rowan insisted that he would only do it if it was an interesting and original character – not just a re-run of somebody he'd played on television before.' Well, it wasn't quite Mr Bean – Latham had lines to say in between the accidents.

It was a frantic schedule. In three weeks the crew filmed in Egypt, Moscow and Westminster, but this was the kind of rollercoaster Atkinson was now on. It was hard to take a break when he was in such demand and the ads had to be fitted in between shooting schedules for

Always keeping an eye out for the future, Atkinson considers his next move.

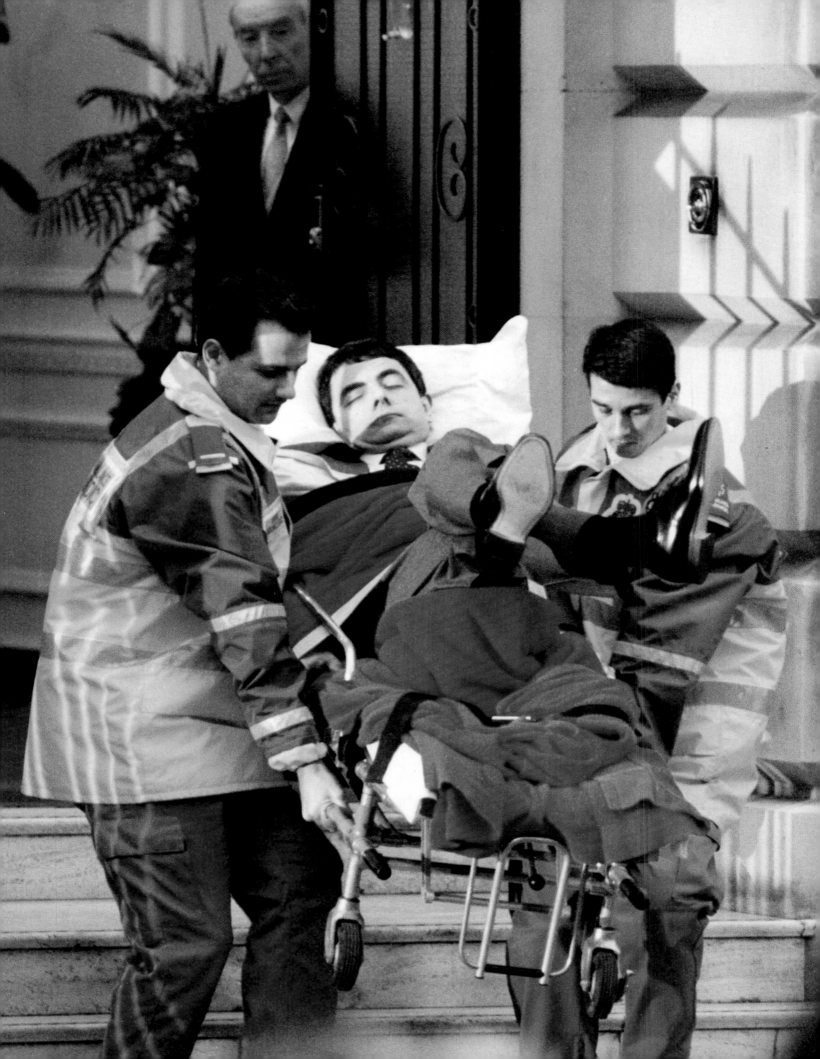

Bean attempts the dating game with limited success.

television programmes. It was worth it, however. Latham would prove to be as durable a character as Mr Bean and, over a series of consistently entertaining ads, if not almost as lucrative as the ITV series, it was certainly not financially insignificant.

Things were hardly likely to get easier on the schedule front. He was also filming an appearance in *The Genie*, a BBC comedy written by Richard Curtis and co-starring Lenny Henry; and in September 1991 it was reported in the *Daily Star* that Atkinson had signed two movie deals with Fox. Would this finally mark his commercial breakthrough in America? Critically he was well established there by 1991. In November of that year Atkinson picked up another Emmy for *The Curse of Mr Bean*, the latest instalment of

oddball misadventures.

Back in Britain, Mr Bean was more popular than ever. Fans wanted to know where the inspiration came from and that autumn he talked frankly about this strange combination of loneliness, childishness and anarchy in the *Daily Mirror*, confirming that it was basically his alter ego, him as a child: 'Not only in the sense of his innocence, but also in his viciousness and vindictiveness when things do not go his way.' Despite the continued success, things didn't come any easier, he explained: 'I hate doing the job of Mr Bean. I find being Mr Bean very stressful. Mr Bean is a very personal comedy statement and there is no support cast.' When things went wrong he didn't lose his temper, he said; he just curled up in a ball.

LEFT
A suitable case for treatment: **filming the adverts for Barclaycard.**

**Meeting
Margaret
Thatcher at
10 Downing
Street**.

RIGHT
All at sea in
Hot Shots
Part Deux.

But this was a disingenuous way of looking at things. Atkinson was so obsessive about his comedy that things had been equally problematic in *Blackadder* when there had been a supporting cast. Anyone who knew the performer would confirm that he contributed substantially to his stress levels himself by trying to get things absolutely perfect. As one Oxford contemporary recalled in *She*, he was just as much of a scientist when he was performing back then, determined to get his equations correct: 'He was infuriating. Everything had to be exactly right – he'd do one little movement over and over, 40 times if necessary, while all the rest of us just had to wait. But the end result was always brilliant.'

Atkinson responded to the accusation claiming, 'I'm not aware that I've ever done anything 40 times – 15 or 20 maybe. I'm aware that I like to get things right and that I have at least a streak of perfectionism.' It wasn't clear whether he was being ironic when he admitted to doing 15 takes – enough to drive any but the most committed supporting cast member to despair. Fortunately Atkinson's track record meant that he could get that

kind of commitment. And no one could say that this scientific approach didn't reap rewards, least of all Atkinson, who agreed that he had had a scientific approach to his comedy: 'No success has ever surprised me. I didn't assume it would happen, but when it came it just seemed logical in relation to applied effort.'

By the end of 1991 Atkinson was a success. *Mr Bean* was a success. Everything he touched turned to gold. Except, that is, Thames Television, the company that had lured him away from the BBC. In the fierce ratings war things got dirty in 1991. Thames Television lost its London television franchise; one of the conspiracy theories was that this was the Tory party's revenge for the station broadcasting *Death on the Rock*, a damning documentary about the killing of suspected IRA terrorists in Gibraltar. *Mr Bean* was caught in the crossfire but inevitably the goose that laid the golden egg wasn't going to die. When Carlton Television took over the franchise on 1 January 1992, *Mr Bean* would continue to be made and go from strength to strength.

Copper-bottomed Success

● ● ● ● ● ● ● ● ● ●

Pulling faces for charity: Red Nose Day 2.

Given Rowan Atkinson's scientific outlook on life, it is surprising that it wasn't until the '90s that he actually applied this analytical sensibility to comedy as a whole rather than just the making of his own comedy. In November 1992 the balance was redressed when his company, Tiger Aspect, made *Funny Business* for the BBC.

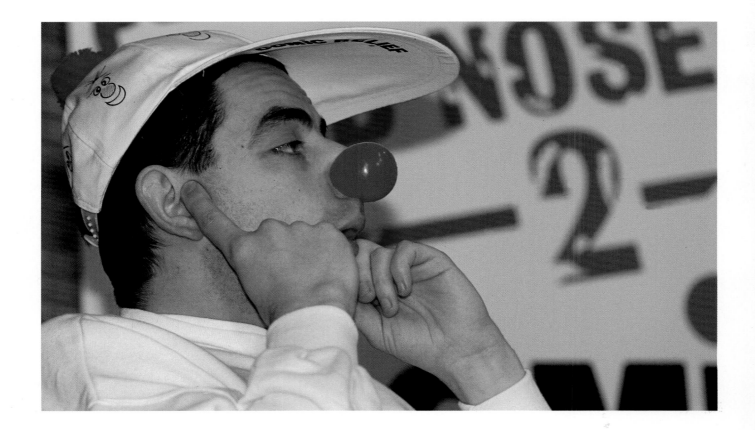

was rushing headlong into a mid-life crisis. He disagreed, but then in many respects he had always seemed middle-aged: 'I don't think I'm in any mid-life crisis, but your perspective shifts as you get into your 40s. Suddenly I have a different view than when I was doing *Not the Nine O'Clock News*.'

As had become the norm, scenes would be rehearsed endlessly until Atkinson felt he had got things right. He admitted he was a perfectionist and conceded that it wasn't such a good thing: 'Perfectionism is more of a disease than a quality. It reduces you to a person who worries too much and that isn't healthy for anyone.' It was something of an achievement that this time round he was only 'healthily nervous' at the prospect of a new project which he considered, with typical middle-class English modesty, to be 'reasonably accomplished. That is not to say it will be popular. You just have to fling it up the flagpole and see if anyone salutes.'

Atkinson had sensibly stuck with someone whose writing he had confidence in, though critics might argue that this is indicative of a fundamental and continuing conservatism in his choice of projects – throughout his career he has always played safe and never gone out on a limb. At the launch of *The Thin Blue Line* he elaborated on the difficulties of constantly coming up with new ideas. 'It is always difficult to know what to do next. It's so much a matter of chance. There are hundreds of extremely talented actors but very few good writers, so we twiddle our thumbs until someone comes up with something suitable.'

Inspector Fowler was the culmination of a succession of parts that had all reflected elements either of Atkinson's own personality or of the world he had grown up in. It was something he acknowledged himself in interviews to promote *The Thin Blue Line*: 'The common link between my parts is that they are establishment – soldiers, vicars, policemen … which must relate significantly to my upbringing.' That he had become a great portrayer of the establishment didn't mean he took it too seriously. Even though he had been known to do readings in his local village church that didn't stop him from mocking the clergy. He had the good sense to know that there is something inherently funny about being British and middle class: 'You can believe in the establishment but by gum, there's a lot to laugh at about it.'

The first series of *The Thin Blue Line* received respectable reviews and respectable viewing figures but it was not a spectacular success. By the time the programme returned a year later, however, some tweaking had worked wonders. It was now screened in the post-watershed slot of 9.30pm, allowing Elton to be that little bit ruder and get back some of the verbal excess that had made *Blackadder* such a winner. The storylines were also a bit sharper and the characters were clichéd yet fully rounded. Atkinson, strangely, seemed to be playing it like a straight man. He didn't even need to do any face-pulling – the young actor James Dreyfus, who played P.C. Goody, seemed to have taken on that mantle, contorting his features and limbs and

Atkinson has always loved a man in uniform: as Inspector Fowler in The Thin Blue Line.

Is it racing driver Sir Henry Birkin or racing fan Rowan Atkinson? Spot the difference.

upstaging the rest of the cast. As Atkinson had learnt from his own hero John Cleese, there was little one can do in front of an audience that can get a big laugh as easily as a silly walk.

When the second series started, Ben Elton conceded in the *Radio Times* that it was hardly a ground-breaking departure, but claimed that that was what would make it a success. While Atkinson thought the idea of a police station was pretty unoriginal, that was what attracted the writer to it: 'In comedy the obvious is often very good. You've got a vast wealth of background knowledge of television police stations that have gone before. You don't have to establish anything. It's just a sitcom full of completely flawed and fumbling but basically decent people.' He was eternally grateful that his old collaborator had agreed to choose his project out of the countless he was regularly offered: 'Thank goodness Rowan said yes. I'm always at it like a terrier, but he's more selective about what he does.' Others might have called Atkinson insecure or reluctant to take risks; working with Elton was another example of sticking with the people he knows – it could be said that the more successful he has become the less inclined he is to take a leap into the complete unknown – but fortunately for Atkinson his old colleagues also happen to be some of the most talented and creative people in the entertainment industry.

The Thin Blue Line shunted Atkinson back into the limelight in Britain, but behind the scenes bigger international deals than ever were being negotiated. The latest Tinseltown tittle-tattle was

that he was being paid £4.5 million by a Hollywood studio to make a Mr Bean movie. Atkinson was certainly making waves in America. In March 1996 he appeared on the *Tonight Show with Jay Leno* and brought his career full circle by shocking a whole new audience with his ancient routine in which he put on his swimming costume without removing his trousers. He then whipped off his trousers in front of Leno and fellow guest David Duchovny of the *X-Files* to reveal a pair of tartan trunks. Some might have read the gesture as a rude response to theatre critic Frank Rich; Atkinson preferred to see it as a tribute to his co-star in *Four Weddings and a Funeral*. 'Englishmen love to take their trousers off – ask Hugh Grant,' said Atkinson, referring to his *Four Weddings* colleague's recent run-in with the Los Angeles Police Department.

It was an old trick but one that went down a storm; a defining moment that cemented Atkinson's relationship with America. After the disappointments on Broadway he had become a player again. There was talk of his appearing as fellow northerner Stan Laurel in a biopic, gossip about his shows, and acclaim as a cross between Benny Hill and Jim Carrey. But while the ubiquitous rumour mills ground into action and the real Rowan Atkinson retreated back behind the high trees of his Oxfordshire rectory, the reality of a Mr Bean movie finally began to take shape. With his old friend Mel Smith directing, filming started on the movie version of Mr Bean, now simply called *Bean*, on 1 September 1996. The action started as Atkinson meant it to

carry on, with his creation wreaking havoc in Harrods. A month later he had crossed the Atlantic and was causing heads to turn while wobbling on a skateboard on Venice Beach. It was an indication of the groundswell of support for Mr Bean that while *Baywatch* was being filmed further down the coast, the crowds were gathered around this unlikely Englishman.

LEFT
Bean goes to America: filming on Venice Beach.

Skating into trouble on the set of Bean.

Rowan Atkinson had come a long
way from his father's farm near
Newcastle. The weather might have
been better, the accents might have
been different, but in the middle
of the mêlée was the same person.
The quintessential Englishman.
The quintessential clown.